TIRAΝA

TRAVEL GUIDE

Discover Tirana: Maps, Directions,
Culture, Top Attractions, Accommodations,
Airports, Banks, The Does & Don'ts,
Restaurants, Festivals, Culinary, Itinerary,
Nightlife & others

JOHN P. WADE

DISCLAIMER

ABOUT THE AUTHOR

John P. Wade, a native of the United States and a resident of North America, is a dedicated travel guide author with a passion for exploring the world's wonders. With a loving family by his side, he navigates the globe, immersing himself in diverse cultures and sharing his travel expertise to promote the joy of travel and tourism.

Married and a proud parent, John understands the importance of family adventures and brings this perspective into his travel guides. His insights resonate with fellow travelers, offering a unique blend of practical advice and heartfelt experiences.

In addition to his role as a travel guide, John is a voracious reader, finding inspiration in the pages of books from around the world. He channels his creativity into making music, capturing the essence of his journeys through melodies that resonate with the soul. His love for laughter is evident in his talent for crafting jokes, adding a touch of humor to his interactions and writings.

For travel enthusiasts seeking more than just destinations, John P. Wade offers a holistic approach to exploration. Through his travel guides, he not only guides you to picturesque locations but also invites you to experience the joy of travel with your loved ones. Embark on a journey of discovery and laughter with John, where every adventure becomes a cherished memory.

TABLE OF CONTENT

INTRODUCTION

Destination Overview

Nestled between the rugged landscapes of Albania, Tirana beckons with an irresistible blend of history, culture, and contemporary charm. As the heart of the nation, this vibrant city pulsates with life, inviting intrepid travelers to unravel its tales of resilience and rebirth. Picture a kaleidoscope of colors adorning the streets, where Ottoman-era relics stand proudly alongside modern masterpieces. In this captivating guide, we unravel the layers of Tirana's narrative, from its storied past to the eclectic present, promising adventurers an odyssey filled with discovery and the promise of unforgettable moments.

Brief History

Tirana's history reads like a tapestry woven with threads of conquest, resilience, and resurgence. Founded in the early 17th century, this city nestled between Dajti Mountain and the coastal plains has endured centuries of Ottoman rule, leaving an indelible mark on its architectural landscape. In the late 20th century, Tirana transformed dramatically, shedding its isolationist cloak to emerge as the vibrant capital of an independent Albania.

The city's central square, Skanderbeg Square, pays homage to the national hero Gjergj Kastrioti, known as Skanderbeg, who led a valiant resistance against the Ottoman Empire in the 15th century. Remnants of communist-era buildings, including the iconic Pyramid of Tirana, serve as tangible reminders of the country's more recent past.

Geography and Climate

Tirana's geographic setting is as diverse as its history. Surrounded by hills and mountains, the city enjoys a picturesque backdrop, with the Dajti Mountain providing a breathtaking panorama. The Lana River meanders through the city, enhancing its scenic allure.

The climate of Tirana is Mediterranean, characterized by hot, dry summers and mild, wet winters. The city's parks and green spaces come alive in the warmer months, offering a refreshing contrast to the bustling urban life. Dajti National Park, accessible by a cable car, provides an escape to nature just a short ride away from the city center.

Culture and Custom

Tirana's cultural landscape is a mosaic of influences, reflecting its rich history and diverse heritage. The city boasts a thriving arts scene, with galleries and theaters showcasing both traditional and contemporary Albanian creations. The National Gallery of Arts stands as a testament to the country's creative spirit.

Albanian hospitality, a cornerstone of local culture, is evident in the city's vibrant cafes and restaurants. Visitors are encouraged to partake in the ritual of sipping Turkish coffee while engaging in lively conversations. Traditional folk music and dance, often performed during festivals, provide a rhythmic insight into the soul of Albanian customs.

Respect for elders and a strong sense of community underscore Tirana's social fabric. Whether exploring the historic neighborhoods of Blloku or engaging in the lively bustle of the New Bazaar, travelers will find themselves enveloped in the warmth of Tirana's cultural embrace, where every street corner holds a story waiting to be shared.

CHAPTER ONE

Maps and Directions

Maps and Key Areas

Navigating the enchanting labyrinth of Tirana becomes a seamless adventure with the aid of detailed maps that unravel the city's diverse districts and key areas. Here, every corner unveils a different facet of the city's character, each neighborhood a unique chapter in Tirana's story.

Skanderbeg Square

At the heart of Tirana, Skanderbeg Square stands as a symbolic epicenter. Bounded by grand government buildings, the square pays homage to Albania's national hero, Skanderbeg. Visitors can explore the equestrian statue of Skanderbeg, the Et'hem Bey Mosque, and the National History Museum, all within this historic square.

Blloku

Once a restricted area during the communist era, Blloku has transformed into Tirana's trendsetting district. Lined with boutiques, cafes, and vibrant street art, Blloku exudes a youthful energy. It's the perfect place to experience Tirana's evolving urban culture, whether shopping for local designer fashion or savoring international cuisine.

The New Bazaar (Pazari i Ri)

A culinary and cultural hub, the New Bazaar beckons with an array of fresh produce, local delicacies, and artisanal crafts. This bustling market is where locals and visitors converge to indulge in the authentic flavors of Albanian cuisine, from traditional pastries to aromatic spices. The vibrant atmosphere makes it a must-visit for those seeking a genuine taste of Tirana.

Dajti Mountain

Escape the urban rhythm and ascend the Dajti Mountain, offering a panoramic retreat just outside the city. Accessible by cable car, the mountain provides sweeping views of Tirana and the surrounding landscape. Dajti National Park, with its hiking trails and diverse flora, invites nature enthusiasts to explore its pristine beauty.

Artificial Lake Park

For a tranquil respite, the Artificial Lake Park offers a serene escape. The expansive lake, surrounded by lush greenery, is a favorite spot for locals and visitors alike. Walking and biking paths wind around the lake, providing a peaceful setting for leisurely strolls or picnics.

Historic Neighborhoods

Tirana's charm is amplified in its historic neighborhoods like *Myslym Shyri* and *Petro Nini Luarasi.* Myslym Shyri boasts a mix of architectural styles, showcasing the city's evolution. Petro Nini Luarasi, named after an Albanian poet, offers a glimpse into the residential life of Tirana with its narrow streets and colorful buildings.

With these key areas on the map, navigating Tirana becomes an exploration of its diverse character, each neighborhood contributing a unique note to the symphony of this captivating city.

Travel Resources and Websites

Embarking on a journey to Tirana is made smoother and more enriching with an array of travel resources and websites that cater to every aspect of planning, exploration, and immersion into the city's vibrant tapestry.

1. Visit Tirana Official Website

The [Visit Tirana] (view here) website serves as the official guide to the city. Packed with comprehensive information, it's a one-stop hub for exploring attractions, events, accommodations, and practical travel tips. The regularly updated blog section provides insights into local culture, festivals, and hidden gems.

2. Tirana International Airport (TIA)

For those flying into Tirana, the [TIA website] (view here) offers essential information about flights, services, and transportation options from the airport to the city center. It ensures a smooth transition for visitors arriving in the Albanian capital.

3. Accommodation Booking Platforms

Platforms like [*Booking.com*] (view here) and [*Airbnb*] (view here) offer a plethora of accommodation options, ranging from boutique hotels to cozy apartments. Users can filter choices based on preferences, read reviews, and secure bookings, ensuring a comfortable stay tailored to individual preferences.

4. Transportation Services

Navigating Tirana and its surroundings is made convenient with transportation services like [*Uber*] (view here) and [*Bolt*] (view here). These apps provide hassle-free rides within the city, allowing travelers to explore with ease.

5. Local Events and Activities

[*Eventbrite*] (view here) and [*Meetup*] (view here) are valuable resources for discovering local events, cultural activities, and gatherings. Whether it's a music festival, art exhibition, or a language exchange meet-up, these platforms enhance the opportunity to engage with Tirana's dynamic community.

6. Travel Forums and Communities

Websites such as *[Lonely Planet's Thorn Tree]* (view here) and *[TripAdvisor Forums]* (view here) offer a platform for travelers to share experiences, seek advice, and connect with fellow explorers. These forums provide real-time insights and recommendations, adding a communal aspect to travel planning.

7. Currency and Banking Information

Understanding the local currency and banking facilities is crucial. Websites like [*XE*] (view here) provide up-to-date currency conversion rates, while [*Revolut*] (views here) and [*TransferWise*] (view here) offer convenient solutions for managing finances while abroad.

8. Language Learning Platforms

To enrich the travel experience, language learning platforms like [*Duolingo*] (view here) can be invaluable. Learning basic Albanian phrases enhances communication and fosters a deeper connection with the local culture.

By leveraging these travel resources and websites, visitors to Tirana can seamlessly plan their journey, immerse themselves in the local experience, and make the most of their exploration in this captivating city.

Recommended Tour Operators

Exploring Tirana and its surrounding treasures is enhanced by engaging with experienced tour operators who offer curated experiences, local insights, and the convenience of guided exploration. Here are some recommended tour operators that ensure travelers make the most of their visit to this captivating city:

1. Albania Express Travel

Albania Express Travel (view here) specializes in creating personalized itineraries that showcase the best of Tirana and beyond. From historical tours of the city center to excursions in the Albanian Riviera, their knowledgeable guides provide a deep understanding of the country's culture and history.

2. Tirana Free Tour

For budget-conscious travelers seeking an immersive experience, *Tirana Free Tour* (view here) offers walking tours led by local guides. The tours cover Skanderbeg Square, Blloku, and other key areas, providing insights into Tirana's history, culture, and daily life.

3. Adventure and Fun Albania

Adventure and Fun Albania (view here) caters to thrill-seekers looking to combine adventure with cultural exploration. From hiking in Dajti National Park to exploring underground bunkers, their diverse range of tours offers a unique perspective on Tirana and its surroundings.

4. Europe Adventure Tours

Europe Adventure Tours (view here) provides comprehensive packages that include Tirana in broader Balkan itineraries. These tours often explore UNESCO World Heritage sites, national parks, and cultural landmarks, offering a holistic experience for those eager to delve into the region's history.

5. GAT Tours

GAT Tours (view here) focuses on introducing travelers to the authentic side of Albania. Their Tirana city tours cover not only the iconic landmarks but also lesser-known gems, ensuring a well-rounded understanding of the city's evolution and culture.

6. Caravan Albania

Caravan Albania (view here) specializes in tailor-made itineraries that cater to individual preferences. Whether it's a culinary tour through Tirana's markets or a historical exploration of the city's landmarks, their flexibility allows visitors to shape their ideal Albanian adventure.

7. Cultural Albania

Cultural Albania (view here) emphasizes cultural immersion through its tours. From traditional folklore performances to visits to local artisans, their itineraries provide a deep dive into Tirana's cultural heritage, fostering a connection with the traditions that define the city.

8. Tirana Ekspres Bike Tours

Tirana Ekspres (view <u>here</u>) offers a unique perspective with its bike tours. Exploring Tirana on two wheels, visitors can cover more ground while experiencing the city's vibrant street art scene and parks. This eco-friendly approach aligns with Tirana's commitment to sustainability.

Engaging with these recommended tour operators ensures that every aspect of Tirana's charm, from its historical significance to its modern vibrancy, is expertly unveiled. Whether seeking adventure, cultural immersion, or a leisurely exploration, these operators cater to diverse preferences, promising an enriching journey through the heart of Albania.

Important Phone Numbers and Contacts

Ensuring a smooth and secure stay in Tirana involves having access to essential phone numbers and contacts. From emergency services to local assistance, these contacts provide travelers with the necessary support for a worry-free experience:

1. Emergency Services

- Emergency Hotline: **112**

- Police: **129**

- Ambulance: **127**

- Fire Department: **128**

For any urgent situations, these emergency numbers are vital. The **112** hotline is a general emergency number that can connect you to police, medical, or fire services.

2. Tourist Information

- Tourist Information Center: **+355 4 225 4880**

- Visit Tirana Information Line: **0800 8001** *(toll-free in Albania)*

Reach out to the Tourist Information Center for guidance on attractions, events, and general inquiries. The Visit Tirana Information Line is a convenient resource for immediate assistance during your stay.

3. Airport and Transportation

- Tirana International Airport (TIA) Information: **+355 4 2381 600**

- Taxi Service (TAXI TIRANA): **+355 69 20 44 777**

If you need information about flights, airport services, or reliable taxi options, these contacts will prove valuable.

4. Medical Assistance

- Emergency Medical Service: **127**

- Ambulance Service (Red Cross): **+355 4 2370 950**

In case of medical emergencies, dial the emergency medical service or contact the Red Cross for ambulance assistance.

5. Embassies and Consulates

Foreign Embassies in Tirana: Contact details can be obtained from the Ministry of Foreign Affairs or respective embassy websites.

- Albanian Ministry of Foreign Affairs: **+355 4 228 7080**

For consular assistance or information about your home country's representation, these contacts are crucial.

6. Lost or Stolen Items

- Police (for reporting lost or stolen items): **129**

If you encounter issues like lost belongings, contact the police to report the incident promptly.

7. Public Services

- Municipality of Tirana: **+355 4 222 3073**

- Public Transport Information: **141**

For city-related services and public transport inquiries, these contacts will be helpful.

8. Utilities and Emergencies

- Water Emergency Service: **+355 69 202 1930**

- Electricity Emergency Service: **+355 67 20 20 235**

In case of utility-related issues or emergencies, these contacts offer assistance.

Having these important phone numbers readily available ensures that travelers in Tirana can promptly access the assistance and information they may need, contributing to a safe and enjoyable visit to this vibrant city.

CHAPTER TWO

Planning Your Trip to Tirana

Best Time to Visit Tirana

Choosing the optimal time to explore Tirana is pivotal to experiencing the city's diverse offerings to the fullest. The Albanian capital enjoys a *Mediterranean climate,* providing distinct seasons that cater to various preferences. The following factors should be considered when planning your visit:

1. Spring (March to May)

Weather: Spring heralds the awakening of nature in Tirana. Mild temperatures, ranging from 10°C to 20°C (50°F to 68°F), create a comfortable atmosphere for outdoor exploration.

Floral Blooms: The city's parks and green spaces come to life with vibrant blossoms, making it an ideal time for nature enthusiasts.

2. Summer (June to August)

Weather: Summer in Tirana is warm and sunny, with temperatures ranging from 20°C to 32°C (68°F to 90°F). This is the peak tourist season, attracting visitors with the promise of long days filled with sunshine.

Festivals and Events: Numerous cultural events, outdoor festivals, and concerts take place during the summer months, offering a lively atmosphere.

3. Autumn (September to November)

Weather: As temperatures gradually cool down, ranging from 10°C to 25°C (50°F to

77°F), autumn provides a pleasant climate for sightseeing. The fall foliage adds a touch of warmth to the city's landscapes.

Cultural Events: Autumn sees a continuation of cultural festivities, and with fewer tourists, it's an excellent time for a more intimate experience.

4. Winter (December to February)

Weather: Winters in Tirana are mild, with temperatures averaging between 2°C and 12°C (36°F to 54°F). While it's the coldest season, snowfall is infrequent in the city.

Festive Atmosphere: The holiday season brings a festive ambiance to Tirana. Decorated streets, Christmas markets, and cultural events make it a charming time to visit.

Considerations for Traveling

Crowd Levels: Summer attracts the highest number of tourists, leading to crowded attractions and accommodations. If you prefer a quieter experience, spring and autumn offer a more serene environment.

Outdoor Activities: Spring and autumn are ideal for outdoor activities, such as hiking in Dajti National Park or exploring the city's parks. Summer is perfect for enjoying the Adriatic Sea beaches, which are easily accessible from Tirana.

Cultural Experiences: Tirana's cultural calendar is vibrant throughout the year, with festivals, art exhibitions, and performances. Checking the event calendar can help align your visit with specific cultural highlights.

Ultimately, the best time to visit Tirana depends on your preferences, whether you seek the lively energy of summer festivals, the colorful landscapes of autumn, or a quieter exploration during the shoulder seasons. Each season unveils a different facet of Tirana's charm, ensuring a memorable experience whenever you choose to embark on your Albanian adventure.

Tirana Travel Budgeting

Crafting a well-thought-out budget is crucial for a rewarding and stress-free experience in Tirana. The city offers a diverse range of experiences, from affordable street food to high-end dining, and budget-friendly accommodations to luxurious hotels. Here's a comprehensive guide to help you plan your travel budget for Tirana:

1. Accommodation

Budget Accommodation: Hostels and guesthouses in Tirana offer economical options, with prices ranging from **$15 to $40** per night.

Mid-Range Hotels: Three-star hotels and boutique accommodations are available in the range of **$40 to $100** per night.

Luxury Hotels: For those seeking luxury, high-end hotels may cost upwards of **$100** per night.

2. Meals

Street Food and Cafes: Enjoying local street food and cafes is a cost-effective way to savor Albanian cuisine. Meals are from **$5 to $15** per person.

Mid-Range Restaurants: Dining in mid-range restaurants may cost between **$15 to $30** per person, offering a more extensive menu and a comfortable ambiance.

Fine Dining: High-end restaurants with gourmet offerings may exceed **$30** per person.

3. Transportation

Public Transport: Public buses and mini-busses are affordable, with fares around **$0.30 to $0.50** per ride.

Taxis: Taxis are readily available, and fares start at around **$2**, with additional charges based on distance.

Car Rentals: Renting a car can be economical, with daily rates starting at **$25**. Gasoline prices are around **$1.50** per liter.

4. Attractions and Activities

Museums and Landmarks: Entrance fees to museums and landmarks vary but generally range from **$2 to $10.**

Tours and Excursions: Guided tours and excursions can range from **$20 to $50**, depending on the duration and included activities.

5. Miscellaneous

SIM Card and Data Plans: Purchasing a local SIM card with data plans is affordable, with options starting at **$5**.

Tips and Tipping Culture: Tipping is appreciated but not mandatory. Leaving a **10%** tip in restaurants is common.

Souvenirs and Shopping: Budget for souvenirs and shopping, keeping in mind that prices vary. Traditional crafts and souvenirs can range from a few dollars to higher-end items.

6. Budget-Friendly Tips

Free Activities: Take advantage of free activities, such as exploring Skanderbeg Square, wandering through parks, and enjoying street art.

Local Markets: Visit local markets for affordable produce, snacks, and a taste of everyday life.

Water: Tap water is generally safe to drink, saving on the cost of bottled water.

7. Currency Exchange

The official currency is the Albanian lek (ALL). Currency exchange services are available, and major credit cards are widely accepted.

8. Travel Insurance

Consider investing in travel insurance to cover unexpected expenses like medical emergencies or trip cancellations.

By tailoring your budget to your preferences and travel style, Tirana can be an affordable destination offering a rich tapestry of experiences. Whether you're a budget-conscious traveler or seeking a more luxurious escape, Tirana accommodates a range of budgets, ensuring an enjoyable visit for every type of explorer.

Tirana Visa and Travel Requirements

Before embarking on your journey to Tirana, it's essential to familiarize yourself with the visa and travel requirements to ensure a smooth and hassle-free visit. Here's a comprehensive guide to Tirana's visa and travel requirements:

1. Visa Requirements

Visa-Free Countries: Citizens of many countries, including the European Union, the United States, Canada, Australia, and several others, can enter Albania for short stays (up to 90 days within a 180-day period) without a visa.

Visa on Arrival: Some nationalities that do not fall under the visa-free category may be eligible for a visa on arrival. It's essential to check specific requirements and eligibility criteria.

2. Passport Requirements

At least three months beyond your intended departure date from Albania, your passport should be valid.

3. Visa Extensions

If you wish to extend your stay beyond the initially granted period, it's advisable to contact local immigration authorities for information on the extension process.

4. Entry and Exit Points

Ensure you enter and exit Albania through official border points and airports. Crossing into or out of the country through unofficial border crossings is illegal and may result in penalties.

5. Health and Insurance

While there are no specific vaccination requirements for entering Albania, it's advisable to be up-to-date on routine vaccinations. Travel insurance, including medical coverage, is highly recommended.

6. Currency Regulations

There are no restrictions on the amount of foreign currency you can bring into Albania. It's advisable to declare amounts over **10,000 euros** or the equivalent in other currencies.

7. Customs Regulations

Be aware of customs regulations, including duty-free allowances. It's prohibited to export antiques and items of cultural significance without proper authorization.

8. Transportation Tickets

Immigration authorities may request proof of onward travel, so having a return ticket or evidence of your travel plans out of Albania is advisable.

9. Local Laws and Regulations

Familiarize yourself with local laws and regulations to ensure you adhere to cultural norms and legal requirements.

10. Emergency Contacts

Keep a list of emergency contacts, including the contact information for your country's embassy or consulate in Tirana.

11. Currency and Payments

The official currency is the Albanian lek (ALL). Credit cards are widely accepted in urban areas, but it's advisable to have some cash, especially in more rural areas.

Note: Regulations can change, and it's crucial to check with the Albanian embassy or consulate in your country or the official Albanian government website for the most up-to-date information before your trip.

By ensuring you meet all visa and travel requirements, you set the stage for a seamless and enjoyable exploration of Tirana and its surroundings.

Health and Safety Tips for Tirana Travel

Ensuring your well-being and safety is paramount when exploring Tirana. The city offers a welcoming environment, but like any travel destination, it's essential to be mindful of health and safety considerations. Here's a comprehensive guide to help you stay healthy and safe during your visit:

1. Medical Preparations

Travel Insurance: Get complete/understandable travel insurance that covers trip cancellations, medical emergencies and other unforeseen events.

Health Checkup: Visit your healthcare provider before traveling to ensure you are up-to-date on routine vaccinations and discuss any specific health concerns.

2. COVID-19 Considerations

Check Entry Requirements: Stay informed about any specific COVID-19 related entry requirements, including testing and quarantine regulations.

Follow Local Guidelines: Adhere to local health and safety guidelines, including mask-wearing and social distancing.

3. Stay Hydrated and Sun-Protected

Water: Drink bottled or purified water to stay hydrated. Avoid tap water unless it's explicitly stated to be safe.

Sun Protection: Tirana has a Mediterranean climate, so use sunscreen, wear protective clothing, and stay hydrated, especially during the warmer months.

4. Food and Hygiene

Local Cuisine: Enjoy the diverse Albanian cuisine, but be cautious with street food.

Engage with vendors and Restaurants with good hygiene practices.

Hand Hygiene: Practice regular handwashing, and carry hand sanitizer for times when soap and water are not readily available.

5. Transportation Safety

Official Taxis: Use officially marked taxis or reputable ride-sharing services to ensure safe transportation.

Public Transport: Be cautious with personal belongings on public transportation, and use reliable services.

6. Secure Your Belongings

Valuables: Keep valuables, including passports, in a secure location. Use a neck pouch or money belt for added security.

Awareness in Crowds: Be vigilant in crowded areas to avoid pickpocketing. Keep an eye on your belongings, especially in bustling markets and tourist sites.

7. Respect Local Customs

Cultural Sensitivity: Respect local customs and traditions. Ask for permission before taking photos of locals and dress modestly when visiting religious sites.

Language Basics: Learn a few basic phrases in Albanian. Locals appreciate efforts to engage in their language.

8. Know Your Surroundings

Map and Navigation: Carry a map or use navigation apps to familiarize yourself with the city's layout. Stay in well-lit and populated areas, especially at night.

9. Health Precautions

Mosquito Protection: If visiting during warmer months, use insect repellent to protect against mosquitoes.

Medical Facilities: Identify nearby medical facilities and pharmacies in case of any health concerns.

10. Be Informed

Local Laws: Associate yourself with regulations and local laws. Be aware of any travel advisories for the region.

Weather Conditions: Stay informed about weather conditions, especially if you plan on exploring outdoor areas.

By incorporating these health and safety tips into your travel plans, you can maximize your enjoyment of Tirana while minimizing potential risks. Always stay informed, be aware of your surroundings, and embrace the adventure responsibly.

Packing List and Travel Gear for Tirana

Preparing a well-thought-out packing list ensures you have the essentials for a comfortable and enjoyable stay in Tirana. The city's diverse offerings, from historical landmarks to vibrant markets, call for a versatile set of travel gear. Here's a comprehensive guide to help you pack for your Tirana adventure:

1. Clothing

Seasonal Attire

- *Spring/Autumn*: Pack layers, including a light jacket or sweater for cooler evenings.

- *Summer:* Lightweight and breathable clothing for the warm weather.

- *Winter*: A warm jacket and layers for cooler temperatures.

Comfortable Shoes
- Walking shoes for exploring the city's streets and parks.

- Sandals for warmer days or beach excursions.

Modest Attire
- If visiting religious sites, have modest clothing to cover shoulders and knees.

2. Travel Accessories

Daypack or Backpack
- A small daypack for daily excursions, carrying essentials like water, snacks, and a map.

Travel Wallet

- Keep important documents, such as your passport, travel insurance, and tickets, organized and secure.

Money Belt or Neck Pouch
- A discreet way to carry valuables, especially in crowded areas.

3. Electronics

Power Adapter
- A universal adapter for charging your electronic devices.

Camera
- Capture the beauty of Tirana with a camera or smartphone.

Portable Charger
- Ensure your devices stay charged, especially during full-day explorations.

4. Health and Personal Care

First Aid Kit
- Include basic medications, bandages, and any personal prescription medications.

Sunscreen and Sun Protection
- Protect your skin from the Mediterranean sun.

Toiletries
- Travel-sized toiletries, toothbrush, toothpaste, and any personal care items.

5. Practical Gear

Travel Towel
- A quick-drying towel for beach visits or unexpected rain.

Umbrella or Rain Jacket
- Be prepared for rain depending on the season.

Reusable Water Bottle
- Stay hydrated while reducing single-use plastic consumption.

6. Language and Navigation

Language Guide or Translation App
- Learn some basic Albanian phrases or use a translation app.

Map or Navigation App
- Navigate the city with ease.

7. Entertainment

Books or E-reader
- Something to read during downtime or long journeys.

Travel Journal
- Document your experiences and memories.

8. Miscellaneous

Sunglasses and Hat
- Protect yourself from the sun.

Reusable Shopping Bag
- Handy for market visits and reducing plastic usage.

Locks for Luggage
- Secure your belongings, especially if staying in shared accommodations.

9. Local Attire (Optional)

Traditional Albanian Clothing
- Consider bringing a piece of traditional attire to engage more deeply with local customs, especially if attending cultural events.

10. Travel Insurance Documents

Copy of Travel Insurance

- Keep a printed or digital copy of your travel insurance details.

This packing list is adaptable based on your individual needs and the specific activities you plan to engage in while in Tirana. Endeavor to check the weather forecast closer to your travel date and make necessary adjustments. With a well-prepared packing list, you'll be ready to immerse yourself in the vibrant culture and stunning landscapes of Tirana.

CHAPTER THREE

Flights and Central Airports, Transportation within and Detailed Accommodation Options

---

Flights and Central Airports in Tirana

Tirana, as the capital of Albania, is served by its primary international airport, providing convenient access for both domestic and international travelers. Here's an extensive guide to flights and central airports in Tirana:

1. Tirana International Airport Nënë Tereza (TIA)

Address: Ruga Nene Tereza, Rinas 1504, Albania

Phone Number: **+355 4 238 1800**
Website: Click here

Location: Tirana International Airport, commonly known as Nënë Tereza Airport, is situated approximately 17 kilometers northwest of Tirana's city center.

Facilities: TIA is equipped with modern facilities, including duty-free shops, restaurants, car rental services, and currency exchange.

Airlines: Several major airlines operate at TIA, connecting Tirana to numerous European cities. Carriers include Turkish Airlines, Alitalia, Lufthansa, British Airways, and more.

Destinations: TIA serves as a gateway to various destinations in Europe and beyond, making it a central hub for travelers exploring Albania and the surrounding region.

2. Domestic and Regional Connections

Domestic Flights: While TIA primarily handles international flights, domestic flights within Albania are available, connecting Tirana to cities like Vlorë, Shkodër, and others.

Regional Connections: TIA facilitates connections to neighboring countries, strengthening ties with regional destinations in the Balkans.

3. Booking Flights to Tirana

Online Platforms: Utilize online travel platforms to compare and book flights to Tirana. Popular websites like Skyscanner, Expedia, and Google Flights offer comprehensive options.

Airlines' Official Websites: Visit the official websites of airlines serving Tirana for the

most up-to-date flight information and
exclusive deals.

4. Transportation to and from TIA

Taxi Services: Taxis are readily available at
the airport, offering a convenient and quick
way to reach the city center. Ensure you use
authorized taxi services.

Airport Shuttle: Shared shuttle services
provide cost-effective transportation options,
with routes connecting the airport to various
points in Tirana.

Car Rentals: Rental car services are
available at TIA, allowing visitors to explore
Tirana and its surroundings at their own
pace.

5. Tips for a Smooth Airport Experience

Arrival Time: Arrive well in advance of your flight to allow for check-in, security checks, and potential delays.

Currency Exchange: If needed, utilize the currency exchange services at the airport for initial expenses.

Language: English is widely spoken at TIA, making communication with airport staff straightforward.

6. Future Developments

Airport Expansion: Tirana International Airport is undergoing expansion projects to accommodate the growing number of passengers and enhance its facilities.

7. Accessibility to Other Destinations

Road Networks: Tirana's central location in Albania allows for efficient road connections to various destinations, making it a strategic starting point for exploring the country.

Whether you're arriving in Tirana for business or leisure, Tirana International Airport serves as a vital transportation hub, ensuring convenient access to the city and facilitating travel connections to diverse destinations. Stay updated with the latest travel information, and enjoy your journey to Tirana!

Transportation within Tirana

Navigating the streets of Tirana is a diverse and accessible experience, with various transportation options catering to different preferences and budgets. Here's an extensive guide to transportation within Tirana:

1. Public Buses

Overview: Tirana has an extensive public bus network operated by A-Tirana. Buses cover key routes within the city and surrounding areas.

Fares and Tickets: Tickets are affordable and can be purchased directly from the driver or at designated kiosks. Be sure to have small denominations of currency.

Frequency: Buses generally operate on a regular schedule, but it's advisable to check the timetable for specific routes.

2. Minibuses (Furgons)

Overview: Furgons are shared minibuses that serve both urban and suburban routes. They are a popular means of transportation, connecting Tirana to neighboring towns and villages.

Convenience: Furgons depart when full, offering flexibility but potentially leading to wait times. They can be flagged down along their routes.

3. Taxis

Availability: Taxis are readily available throughout Tirana. Look for licensed taxi services with clearly marked vehicles.

Fares: Taxi fares are relatively affordable, and it's advisable to confirm the fare with the driver before starting the journey.

Ride-Sharing Apps: Services like Uber and Bolt operate in Tirana, providing an additional convenient and transparent option.

4. Bicycles

Bike Rentals: Tirana is becoming increasingly bike-friendly, with rental services available for those who want to explore the city on two wheels.

Bike Lanes: The city has dedicated bike lanes, offering a safe and scenic way to travel.

5. Walking

Pedestrian-Friendly Areas: The city center, especially around Skanderbeg Square and the Blloku district, is pedestrian-friendly with vibrant streets, shops, and cafes.

Exploration: Many of Tirana's attractions are within walking distance of each other, allowing for leisurely exploration.

6. Car Rentals

Rental Agencies: Several car rental agencies operate in Tirana, offering options for those who prefer the flexibility of self-driving.

Road Conditions: Roads in and around Tirana are generally in good condition, making it convenient to explore the city and venture into the surrounding areas.

7. Rikshaws and Horse-Drawn Carriages

City Tours: For a unique experience, consider taking a rickshaw or a horse-drawn carriage for a city tour, especially in the more historical parts of Tirana.

8. Future Developments

Public Transportation Expansion: Tirana is continually working on improving its public transportation system, with plans for expanding routes and enhancing services.

9. Tips for Getting Around

Traffic Considerations: Tirana can experience traffic congestion, especially during peak hours. Plan travel times accordingly.

Local Currency: Have small denominations of the local currency (Albanian lek) for public buses and minibuses.

Language: While English is not universally spoken, especially in more local areas, locals are often helpful in assisting travelers.

10. Accessibility

Accessibility Features: Tirana is working to improve accessibility for people with mobility challenges. However, it's advisable to check for specific accommodations before traveling.

Whether you prefer the convenience of taxis, the flexibility of walking, or the local flavor of furgons, Tirana offers a variety of transportation options to suit your preferences. Exploring the city's vibrant neighborhoods and cultural attractions is made easy through its diverse and accessible transportation network.

Detailed Accommodation Options in Tirana

Tirana, as the capital of Albania, provides a range of accommodation options catering to various preferences and budgets. From luxury hotels to budget-friendly guesthouses, the city offers a diverse selection of places to stay. Here's an extensive guide to accommodation options in Tirana:

1. Luxury Hotels

- **Plaza Hotel Tirana**

Address: Rruga Abdi Toptani 18, Tiranë 1001, Albania
Phone Number: **+355 4 221 1221**
Price per Night: **$165**
Website: Click here

Location: Situated near the city center, Plaza Hotel Tirana offers a luxurious stay with modern amenities.

Facilities: Features include spacious rooms, a rooftop pool, wellness center, and multiple dining options.

Amenities: Free Wi-Fi, parking, and attentive service.

2. Mid-Range Hotels

• Hotel Theranda

Address: Rruga Andon Zako Çajupi, Tirana, Albania
Phone Number: **+355 69 207 2900**
Price per Night: **$54**
Website: Click here

Location: In the heart of Tirana, Hotel Theranda provides a comfortable stay with a blend of modern and traditional elements.

Facilities: Cozy rooms, a restaurant serving local cuisine, and a terrace for relaxation.

Amenities: Free Wi-Fi, airport shuttle, and helpful staff.

- **Sky Hotel**
Address: Rruga Dëshmorët E 4 Shkurtit, 5/1, Tiranë 1000, Albania
Phone Number: +355 4 241 5995
Price per Night: $91
Website: Click here

Location: Sky Hotel is centrally located, offering easy access to major attractions.

Facilities: Stylish rooms, a rooftop bar, and a restaurant with city views.

Amenities: Fitness center, free parking, and conference facilities.

3. Boutique Hotels

- **Hotel Vila e Arte**

Address: 8RJF+23C, Rruga Qemal Stafa, Tiranë, Albania
Phone Number: +355 68 204 2007
Price per Night: $54
Website: Click here

Location: Set in a quiet area, this boutique hotel features artistic decor and a tranquil atmosphere.

Facilities: Unique rooms, a garden, and an on-site art gallery.

Amenities: Complimentary breakfast, free parking, and a charming courtyard.

- **Kruja Hotel**

Address: Rruga Mine Peza, Tiranë, Albania
Phone Number: +355 4 223 8106
Price per Night: $55
Website: Click here

Location: A boutique hotel located near the vibrant Blloku district.

Facilities: Elegant rooms, a cozy lounge, and a terrace with city views.

Amenities: Free Wi-Fi, airport shuttle, and personalized service.

4. Budget-Friendly Options

- **Trip'n'Hostel**

Address: Rruga Musa Maci 1, Tirana, Albania
Phone Number: **+355 68 304 8905**
Price per Night: **$31**
Website: Click here

Location: Ideal for budget travelers, Trip'n'Hostel is located in a lively area with easy access to attractions.

Facilities: Dormitory and private rooms, communal kitchen, and a social atmosphere.

Amenities: Free breakfast, Wi-Fi, and organized city tours.

- **Hostel Fredi**

Address: Rruga Bardhok Biba, Tiranë, Albania
Phone Number: +355 68 203 5261
Price per Night: $62

Location: A budget-friendly option in the city center, Hostel Fredi provides basic accommodation for travelers on a budget.

Facilities: Dormitory-style rooms, communal areas, and a relaxed environment.

Amenities: Free Wi-Fi, 24-hour reception, and affordable rates.

5. Apartments and Guesthouses

- **Guesthouse London**

Address: 2 Aspland Grove, London E8 1FJ, United Kingdom
Phone Number: +44 20 8629 7884
Price per Night: $44

Location: A charming guesthouse in a residential area, Guesthouse London offers a home-like atmosphere.

Facilities: Comfortable rooms, a garden, and a communal kitchen.

Amenities: Free parking, Wi-Fi, and personalized service.

- **Tirana Boutique Hotel**
Address: Rruga Jul Variboba, Tirana 1010, Albania
Price per Night: **$105**
Website: Click here

Location: Centrally located, Tirana Boutique Hotel offers apartments with a kitchenette, suitable for longer stays.

Facilities: Spacious apartments, a rooftop terrace, and modern amenities.

Amenities: Free breakfast, airport shuttle, and laundry services.

6. Specialty Accommodations

- **Hotel Mak Albania Resort & Spa**
Address: Sheshi Italia 2, Tiranë 1019, Albania
Phone Number: **+355 4 227 4707**

Price per Night: $137
Website: Click here

Location: Located a short drive from Tirana, this resort-style hotel offers a tranquil escape.

Facilities: Spa, outdoor pool, and spacious rooms with scenic views.

Amenities: On-site dining, fitness center, and conference facilities.

- **Art Hotel Rogner**

Address: Golden Eagle Shpk, Bulevardi Dëshmorët e Kombit 9, Tiranë 1010, Albania
Phone Number: +355 4 223 5035
Price per Night: $121
Website: Click here

Location: Set in a historic building, Art Hotel Rogner combines art and hospitality.

Facilities: Art-themed rooms, a garden, and an on-site art gallery.

Amenities: Fine dining restaurant, spa, and event spaces.

When choosing accommodation in Tirana, consider your preferences, budget, and the desired atmosphere. Whether you opt for the luxury of a five-star hotel or the charm of a boutique guesthouse, Tirana provides a variety of options to suit every traveler's needs.

CHAPTER FOUR

Banks, Currency and Payment Methods

Banks in Tirana

Tirana, as the capital city of Albania, hosts a variety of banks and financial institutions. Here's an overview of banking in Tirana:

1. Central Bank of Albania (Banka e Shqipërisë)

- As the country's central bank, the Bank of Albania is responsible for monetary policy and issuing the national currency, the Albanian lek (ALL).

- While it primarily focuses on macroeconomic stability, it plays a crucial role in overseeing the banking sector.

2. Commercial Banks

- Several commercial banks operate in Tirana, offering a range of financial services. Some prominent ones include Raiffeisen Bank, Intesa Sanpaolo Bank, Alpha Bank, and Credins Bank.

- These banks provide services such as savings and checking accounts, loans, and currency exchange.

3. ATMs and Branches

- ATMs are widely available throughout Tirana, allowing visitors to withdraw local currency easily.

- Banking branches are concentrated in the city center, making it convenient for both residents and tourists to access financial services.

4. Currency Exchange

- Banks in Tirana offer currency exchange services, allowing visitors to convert foreign currency to Albanian lek. Additionally, there are independent exchange offices in key areas.

5. Online Banking

- Many banks in Tirana provide online banking services, enabling account holders to manage their finances, transfer funds, and pay bills conveniently.

6. Banking Hours

- Typical banking hours in Tirana are from Monday to Friday, 8:30 AM to 3:30 PM. Some banks may offer limited services on Saturdays.

Currency

Albanians use Albania lek (ALL) as official currency. Here are key details about the currency:

1. Albanian Lek (ALL)

- The lek is abbreviated as **ALL** and is denoted by the symbol **"L."**

- Banknotes and coins are in circulation, with various denominations, including *200, 500, 1,000, 2,000, and 5,000 lekë banknotes.*

2. Currency Exchange

- At banks, some hotels and exchange offices, currency exchange services are available.

- It's advisable to compare rates and fees before exchanging currency to ensure the best value.

3. Credit Card Usage

- Credit cards, especially Visa and MasterCard, are widely accepted in urban areas and larger establishments.

- However, it's advisable to carry cash for transactions in smaller shops, markets, or in more rural areas.

4. ATMs

- ATMs are prevalent in Tirana, allowing visitors to withdraw

Albanian lek with major international credit and debit cards.

- Inform your bank of your travel dates to avoid potential issues with card usage abroad.

Payment Methods in Tirana

Understanding the prevalent payment methods in Tirana enhances your overall travel experience:

1. Cash Transactions

- Cash is commonly used for daily transactions, especially in markets, smaller shops, and for services like taxis.

- Ensure you have sufficient Albanian lek on hand for expenses in places where card payments may not be accepted.

2. Credit and Debit Cards

- Major credit and debit cards, such as Visa and MasterCard, are widely accepted in hotels, restaurants, and larger stores in Tirana.

- To avoid any potential issues with card transactions, notify your bank of your travel plans.

3. Mobile Payments

- Mobile payment options are becoming more prevalent in Tirana. Some establishments may accept mobile payment apps, so check with the merchant in advance.

4. Contactless Payments

- Contactless card payments are increasingly available, providing a convenient and efficient way to make transactions.

5. Traveler's Checks

- While traveler's checks are less commonly used today, some establishments may still accept them. It's recommended to use more widely accepted forms of payment.

6. Currency Conversion Apps

- Consider using currency conversion apps to stay updated on exchange rates and manage your expenses effectively.

Understanding the local payment methods ensures a seamless experience while exploring Tirana. Having a combination of cash and card options provides flexibility for various transactions in the city.

CHAPTER FIVE

Things to See Do and Avoid in Tirana

Top Tourist Attractions in Tirana

Tirana, the vibrant capital of Albania, is a city that seamlessly blends history, culture, and modernity. From historic landmarks to lively neighborhoods, Tirana offers a diverse range of attractions that captivate visitors. Here's an extensive guide to the top tourist attractions in Tirana:

1. Skanderbeg Square
Address: Plaza Tirana, Sheshi Skender Beu, Tirana 1001, Albania

Iconic Center: Skanderbeg Square is the heart of Tirana, surrounded by important buildings like the National History Museum, the Clock Tower, and the Et'hem Bey Mosque.

Monument to Skanderbeg: The square is dominated by a statue of Gjergj Kastrioti Skanderbeg, a national hero who led the resistance against the Ottoman Empire.

2. Bunk'Art 2

Address:
Street Abdi Toptani, Tiranë, Albania
Phone Number: +355 67 207 2905
Website: Click here

Historical Bunker: Housed in a massive nuclear bunker, Bunk'Art 2 is a museum and art gallery that explores Albania's communist history.

Interactive Exhibits: Engaging exhibits provide insight into the country's political past, including the impact of Enver Hoxha's regime.

3. National History Museum
Address: Sheshi Skënderbej 7, Tirana 1001, Albania
Phone Number: +355 4 222 3977
Website: Click here

Cultural Repository: The museum is a comprehensive showcase of Albania's history, featuring artifacts from prehistoric times to the present day.

Mosaic Facade: The distinctive mosaic on the museum's facade depicts significant events and figures from Albanian history.

4. Et'hem Bey Mosque
Address: AL, Sheshi Skënderbej, 1000, Albania

Architectural Gem: Constructed in the late 18th century, this mosque is a masterpiece of Ottoman architecture.

Historical Significance: The mosque survived the atheist campaign during the communist era, making it an important symbol of religious tolerance.

5. Mount Dajti National Park
Address: 9W52+JV2, Tirana, Albania

Nature Escape: Located just outside Tirana, Mount Dajti offers a refreshing retreat with hiking trails, cable car rides, and panoramic views of the city.

Adventure Activities: Visitors can enjoy activities like paragliding and explore the park's diverse flora and fauna.

6. Blloku District

Trendy Neighborhood: Once a restricted area for communist officials, Blloku has transformed into a lively district with trendy cafes, boutiques, and nightlife.

Enver Hoxha's Villa: Enver Hoxha's former residence is now open to the public, providing a glimpse into the dictator's life.

7. National Art Gallery

Address: 8RGC+75F, Tirana, Albania

Artistic Showcase: The National Art Gallery houses an extensive collection of Albanian art, spanning various periods and styles.

Prominent Artists: Works by renowned Albanian artists, including Onufri and Kolë Idromeno, are featured in the gallery.

8. Grand Park (Parku i Madh)

Address: 8R6G+W32, Rruga Herman Gmeiner, Tirana 1000, Albania
Website: Click here

Green Oasis: Grand Park is a sprawling green space with walking paths, lakes, and recreational areas.

Peaceful Retreat: Ideal for a leisurely stroll or a relaxing afternoon, the park offers a peaceful escape from the urban bustle.

9. Pyramid of Tirana

Address: 8RFC+7J, Tirana 1001, Albania
Website: Click here

Architectural Curiosity: Originally built as a museum to honor Enver Hoxha, the Pyramid of Tirana is now an abandoned structure with a unique design.

Street Art Hub: Despite its controversial history, the pyramid has become a canvas for vibrant street art.

10. The New Bazaar (Pazari i Ri)

Culinary Delights: The New Bazaar is a bustling market where locals and tourists alike can explore fresh produce, local crafts, and enjoy traditional Albanian cuisine.

Lively Atmosphere: The market is a vibrant hub that reflects the authentic daily life of Tirana.

11. Tanners' Bridge (Ura e Tabakëve)
Address: Bulevardi "Jean D'Arc, Tirana, Albania
Website: Click here

Historic Bridge: Dating back to the Ottoman era, Tanners' Bridge is a picturesque stone bridge that crosses the Lana River.

Architectural Charm: The bridge's arches and cobbled surroundings provide a charming backdrop for photographs.

Tirana's allure lies in its ability to seamlessly blend the old and the new, offering visitors a rich tapestry of history, culture, and modernity. These top tourist attractions provide a glimpse into the diverse facets of Tirana's identity, making it a compelling destination for exploration.

Off the Beaten Path Experience in Tirana

While Tirana's main attractions are well-known, the city also hides gems off the beaten path, waiting to be discovered by the more adventurous traveler. Here's an extensive guide to off-the-beaten-path experiences in Tirana:

1. The House of Leaves (Shtëpia e Gjetheve)
Address: 8RG8+MHG, Tirana, Albania
Phone Number: +355 4 222 2612
Website: Click here

Secret Surveillance Museum: Tucked away in the Blloku district, this museum reveals the dark history of surveillance during the communist era.

Interactive Exhibits: The museum's exhibits provide a chilling insight into the methods used by the Sigurimi, the secret police.

2. Petrela Castle
Address: Rruga Petreles, Petrelë, Albania
Phone Number: +355 68 231 8333
Website: Click here

Medieval Fortress: Located on a hill overlooking the surrounding landscape, Petrela Castle offers a tranquil escape from the city.

Historical Charm: The castle, dating back to the 15th century, provides a glimpse into Albania's medieval past.

3. Selman Stermasi Stadium
Address: Rruga Gjin Bue Shpata 27, Tirana, Albania

Sports and Street Art Fusion: While the stadium itself is known for football matches, the surrounding area is adorned with vibrant street art.

Local Flavor: Explore the artistic expressions of local and international street artists, transforming this sports hub into an open-air gallery.

4. Tanners' Bridge (Ura e Tabakëve)
Address: Bulevardi "Jean D'Arc, Tirana, Albania

Historic Stone Bridge: Far from the bustling city center, Tanners' Bridge is a charming Ottoman-era bridge spanning the Lana River.

Tranquil Setting: The serene atmosphere and the picturesque surroundings make it an ideal spot for a peaceful stroll.

5. Tirana Lake Park (Parku i Liqenit)

Address: 8R6G+W32, Rruga Herman Gmeiner, Tirana 1000, Albania
Website: Click here

Nature Escape: Adjacent to the artificial lake, this park provides a tranquil retreat for those seeking a break from urban life.

Boat Rides: Enjoy a boat ride on the lake or simply relax by the water, surrounded by lush greenery.

6. The Pyramid of Tirana

Abandoned Architectural Curiosity: Originally designed as a museum for Enver Hoxha, the Pyramid is now an unconventional canvas for street art.

Alternative Perspective: Explore the graffiti-covered structure and witness how locals have transformed it into a unique artistic space.

7. Xhamia e Pazarit (Market Mosque)

Address: 8RJF+2WM, Rruga Thimi Mitko, Tirana, Albania
Website: Click here

Hidden Mosque: Nestled within the old market area, this small mosque is often overlooked by tourists.

Architectural Heritage: Admire the Ottoman architecture and experience a moment of tranquility away from the more frequented sites.

8. Farkë Village

Rural Retreat: Escape the city and visit Farkë, a picturesque village on the outskirts of Tirana.

Countryside Charm: Experience traditional Albanian village life, surrounded by rolling hills and agricultural landscapes.

9. The Art House (Shtëpia e Artit)
Address: 8R46+JQ2, Rruga Eduard Mano, Tiranë, Albania
Phone Number: +355 69 669 3666

Independent Art Space: This creative hub supports emerging artists and hosts exhibitions, workshops, and cultural events.

Local Art Scene: Engage with the thriving contemporary art scene in Tirana beyond the more mainstream galleries.

10. The Artificial Lake of Tirana
Address: 8VCF+GGC, Rruga Lugjasi Poshte Farkë e AL, 1000, Albania
Phone Number: +355666648222

Website: Click <u>here</u>

Local Hangout: Popular among locals for leisurely walks and picnics, the Artificial Lake offers a peaceful atmosphere.

Cafes and Restaurants: Explore the lakeside cafes and restaurants, providing a different perspective of Tirana.

11. Preza Castle
Address: Prezë, Albania

Hilltop Fortress: Located on a hill near Tirana, Preza Castle offers panoramic views of the surrounding landscape.

Historical Significance: The castle has a rich history and is an excellent spot for those seeking a combination of history and nature.

Embark on these off-the-beaten-path experiences in Tirana to uncover hidden treasures, engage with local culture, and enjoy a more intimate connection with this dynamic and evolving city. These lesser-known gems provide a unique perspective that goes beyond the typical tourist trail.

Outdoor Activities in Tirana

Tirana, nestled between hills and surrounded by nature, offers a myriad of outdoor activities for those who seek adventure, tranquility, or a bit of both. Here's an extensive guide to outdoor activities in Tirana:

1. Mount Dajti Hiking and Cable Car

Hiking Trails: Mount Dajti, visible from Tirana, beckons hikers with trails of varying difficulty levels. Choose a route that suits your preference and enjoy breathtaking views of the city and beyond.

Cable Car Ride: For a more leisurely ascent, take the Dajti Express cable car for panoramic views as you ascend to the mountaintop.

2. Artificial Lake of Tirana

Boat Rides: Explore the tranquil waters of the Artificial Lake by renting a rowboat or pedal boat. It's a serene way to spend a relaxing afternoon.

Jogging and Cycling: The lakeside promenade is ideal for jogging, cycling, or simply strolling. Numerous cafes along the shore offer perfect spots to unwind.

3. Grand Park (Parku i Madh)

Nature Trails: Grand Park, adjacent to the Artificial Lake, boasts walking trails that wind through lush greenery. It's a peaceful retreat for nature enthusiasts.

Picnics and Relaxation: Pack a picnic and enjoy a day of relaxation in the park. Several open spaces provide opportunities for outdoor activities and games.

4. Adventure Park at Lake Farka

Ziplining and Climbing: Lake Farka, a short drive from Tirana, hosts an adventure park with ziplining and climbing activities. It's perfect for thrill-seekers and those looking for a bit of adrenaline.

Lake Views: The park's location by the lake adds a scenic backdrop to your adventure.

5. Mount Dajti National Park Cycling

Mountain Biking Trails: Mountain biking enthusiasts will find a network of trails in Mount Dajti National Park. The diverse terrain offers routes for various skill levels.

Guided Tours: Join a guided cycling tour to explore the park's beauty and discover hidden gems.

6. Tujani Canyon Exploration

Canyoning: For an adventurous day trip, head to Tujani Canyon, not far from Tirana. Engage in canyoning activities, including rappelling and swimming through the canyon's water pools.

Natural Wonders: The rugged landscape and natural formations make Tujani Canyon a unique outdoor destination.

7. Dajti Adventure Park

Rope Courses and Zip Lines: Dajti Adventure Park, located on Mount Dajti, offers thrilling rope courses and zip lines amidst the forest canopy.

Family-Friendly: With options for various age groups, it's an excellent choice for families and groups seeking an active day outdoors.

8. Liqeni i Bovillës (Bovilla Lake)

Fishing and Relaxation: Bovilla Lake, surrounded by hills, is a peaceful retreat. Enjoy fishing, take a boat ride, or simply unwind by the lake.

Scenic Drive: The journey to Bovilla Lake itself is scenic, making it a delightful day trip from Tirana.

9. Picnic at Pellumbas Cave

Nature and Archaeology: Pellumbas Cave, not far from Tirana, offers a combination of nature and archaeological exploration. Hike to the cave entrance and enjoy a picnic amid the stunning surroundings.

Cave Tours: Guided tours inside the cave provide insight into its geological and historical significance.

10. Tanners' Bridge Cycling Trail

Cycling Excursion: Explore the outskirts of Tirana on a cycling tour that includes the historic Tanners' Bridge. The route offers a mix of cultural and natural attractions.

Rural Experience: Pass through villages, fields, and enjoy the rural charm while cycling through the countryside.

Whether you prefer the adrenaline rush of adventure sports, the tranquility of lakeside strolls, or the exploration of hidden caves, Tirana's outdoor offerings cater to a diverse range of interests. Embrace the natural beauty and outdoor adventures that make Tirana a dynamic destination for nature enthusiasts and active travelers.

Cultural Experience

Tirana, with its rich history and diverse cultural heritage, provides an immersive experience for those eager to explore its cultural tapestry:

1. National History Museum

Immerse yourself in Albania's past through the National History Museum's exhibits, showcasing artifacts from prehistoric times to the present.

2. Bunk'Art 2

Experience the unique fusion of history and art in a former nuclear bunker. Bunk'Art 2 explores Albania's communist era through interactive exhibits and contemporary art installations.

3. Art Galleries

Explore Tirana's vibrant art scene by visiting galleries like FAB Gallery, showcasing contemporary Albanian art, or the National Gallery of Arts, featuring classical and modern works.

4. Traditional Markets

Dive into local culture by wandering through bustling markets like Pazari i Ri (The New Bazaar), where you can interact with vendors, taste local delicacies, and shop for traditional crafts.

5. Ethnographic Museum

Discover the cultural diversity of Albania at the Ethnographic Museum, housed in a historic villa, with exhibits showcasing traditional clothing, tools, and artifacts.

6. Mosques and Churches

Visit the Et'hem Bey Mosque, an architectural gem, and explore religious diversity by visiting Orthodox and Catholic churches scattered throughout the city.

Events and Festivals

Tirana comes alive with a vibrant calendar of events and festivals throughout the year, celebrating art, music, and cultural diversity:

1. Tirana International Film Festival (TIFF)

Embrace the cinematic arts at TIFF, showcasing international and Albanian films, with screenings, discussions, and awards ceremonies.

2. Tirana Jazz Festival

Jazz enthusiasts can enjoy world-class performances during the Tirana Jazz

Festival, featuring both local and international artists.

3. Tirana Architecture Week
Dive into the world of architecture during this week-long event, featuring lectures, exhibitions, and workshops exploring urban development and design.

4. Summer Festival
Celebrate summer with the Tirana Summer Festival, offering a diverse program of concerts, outdoor events, and cultural activities in various city locations.

5. Tirana Beer Fest
Beer aficionados can savor local and international brews at the Tirana Beer Fest, accompanied by live music and a lively atmosphere.

Family-Friendly Activities

Tirana provides an array of family-friendly activities, ensuring an enjoyable experience for visitors of all ages.

Dajti Ekspres Cable Car
Take the cable car to Mount Dajti for stunning views and family-friendly activities, including playgrounds, nature trails, and picnic areas.

Amusement Parks
Visit Kidzania Tirana or the Luna Park for a day of family fun, with rides, games, and entertainment suitable for children of various ages.

Tirana Zoo
Explore the Tirana Zoo, home to a variety of animals, and enjoy a leisurely day surrounded by nature and wildlife.

Bicycle Tours

Discover the city on two wheels with family-friendly bicycle tours, exploring parks, boulevards, and cultural landmarks.

Puppet Theater
Attend a performance at the Puppet Theater, offering entertaining and educational shows for children in a lively and interactive setting.

7 Days Itinerary Plan

Plan a week-long exploration of Tirana with a diverse itinerary that covers cultural, historical, and outdoor experiences:

Day 1-2: Historical Exploration

- Explore Skanderbeg Square, visit the National History Museum, and discover the Et'hem Bey Mosque.

Stroll through the historic neighborhoods of Blloku and visit the House of Leaves museum.

Day 3-4: Nature and Adventure

- Take a cable car ride to Mount Dajti for hiking and outdoor activities. Visit the Adventure Park at Lake Farka for ziplining and climbing adventures.

Day 5-6: Cultural Immersion

- Explore art galleries such as FAB Gallery and the National Gallery of Arts. Experience the vibrant local culture at Pazari i Ri and indulge in traditional Albanian cuisine.

Day 7: Relaxation and Family Fun

- Spend a leisurely day at the Artificial Lake, enjoying boat rides and lakeside activities. Visit Kidzania Tirana or

Luna Park for family-friendly entertainment.

Things to Avoid

While Tirana is generally a safe and welcoming destination, there are a few considerations to enhance your travel experience:

Unofficial Money Changers
Avoid exchanging currency with unofficial street money changers. Use reputable banks or exchange offices for secure transactions.

Traffic Safety
Exercise caution when crossing streets, as traffic can be busy. Use designated crosswalks and be aware of local driving habits.

Nighttime Vigilance

Be mindful of your surroundings, especially at night. Stick to well-lit areas and avoid poorly lit or isolated streets.

Street Demonstrations

Stay informed about local events and demonstrations. While Tirana is generally peaceful, it's advisable to avoid areas where large gatherings or protests are taking place.

Waste Disposal

Be mindful of waste disposal practices. Use designated bins and avoid littering to contribute to the city's cleanliness.

By considering these tips, you can make the most of your time in Tirana, ensuring a safe and enjoyable travel experience. Explore the city's cultural richness, partake in local festivities, and savor the diverse experiences this vibrant capital has to offer.

CHAPTER SIX

Eating and Drinking

Tirana Restaurants

Tirana's dining scene is a delightful fusion of traditional Albanian flavors, international cuisines, and modern culinary innovation. Here's an extensive guide to the diverse range of restaurants that make up the gastronomic landscape of Tirana:

1. Mullixhiu

Address: Shëtitorja Lasgush Poradeci Hyrja e Parkut tek Diga e Liqenit Artificial Tirana, 1019, Albania
Phone Number: **+355 69 666 0444**
Menu: Click here
Website: Click here

Culinary Excellence: Mullixhiu, led by renowned chef Bledar Kola, offers a fine dining experience that celebrates Albanian ingredients and culinary traditions.

Signature Dishes: Indulge in dishes like "Tave Kosi" with a modern twist or the chef's tasting menu for a journey through Albanian flavors.

2. Oda
Address: Rruga Shenasi Dishnica, Tirana, Albania
Phone Number: +355 69 204 0145
Menu: Click here

Historic Ambiance: Located in a beautifully restored Ottoman-era building, Oda provides an intimate setting to savor traditional Albanian cuisine.

Local Ingredients: The menu features dishes crafted with locally sourced ingredients, highlighting the rich culinary heritage of the region.

3. Pellumbas Restaurant

Address: 6XV4+C38, Pëllumbas, Albania
Phone Number: +355 68 264 7414

Scenic Setting: Nestled near Pellumbas Cave, this restaurant offers a picturesque setting with views of nature. It's an ideal spot for a relaxing meal after exploring the nearby attractions.

Fresh Seafood: Pellumbas Restaurant is known for its fresh seafood dishes and a diverse menu inspired by Albanian culinary traditions.

4. Era Restaurant

Address: Rruga Papa Gjon Pali II, Tirana, Albania
Phone Number: +355 68 902 4561
Website: Click here

Panoramic Views: Situated on the 9th floor, Era Restaurant provides stunning panoramic views of Tirana. The modern and elegant ambiance complements the diverse menu.

International Cuisine: With a menu featuring a mix of international and Albanian dishes, Era Restaurant is a popular choice for those seeking a sophisticated dining experience.

5. Serendipity Wine and Coffee Bar
Address: Rruga Ibrahim Rugova, Kati i 1-re, Tirana, Albania
Phone Number: +355 68 902 8029

Wine Connoisseur's Haven: Serendipity is a haven for wine enthusiasts, offering an extensive selection of local and international wines. The cozy atmosphere is perfect for both casual and intimate gatherings.

Artisanal Coffee: Additionally, coffee lovers can indulge in a range of artisanal coffee blends, creating a unique blend of flavors.

6. Salt
Address: Rruga Pjetër Bogdani, Tiranë 1001, Albania
Phone Number: +355 69 400 0013
Website: Click here

Modern Mediterranean Cuisine: Salt, located in the heart of Tirana, combines Mediterranean flavors with a modern twist. The menu features a diverse selection of dishes prepared with fresh, seasonal ingredients.

Chic Design: The restaurant's chic design and contemporary atmosphere make it a popular choice for those seeking a stylish dining experience.

7. Artigiano

Address: Rruga Papa Gjon Pali II 9, Tirana 1001, Albania
Phone Number: +355 67 600 0480
Website: Click here

Italian Flair: For lovers of Italian cuisine, Artigiano offers an authentic experience with a menu featuring classic pasta dishes, wood-fired pizzas, and flavorful antipasti.

Warm Atmosphere: The warm and welcoming atmosphere, coupled with a wide selection of Italian wines, creates a cozy and enjoyable dining environment.

8. Mishri Mbi Qepë

Address: Rruga Sami Frashëri, Tirana 1001, Albania
Phone Number: **+355 69 911 1180**
Website: Click here

Grilled Delights: As the name translates to "meat on the grill," Mishri Mbi Qepë is a haven for carnivores. The restaurant specializes in grilled meats, served with a variety of side dishes.

Alfresco Dining: Enjoy alfresco dining in the outdoor garden area, creating a relaxed and convivial atmosphere.

9. Juvenilja

Address: Rruga Sami Frashëri, Tirana, Albania
Phone Number: +355 4 227 2222

Historical Charm: Established in 1920, Juvenilja is one of Tirana's oldest restaurants, known for its historical charm and classic Albanian dishes.

Live Music: Guests can enjoy live music performances as they savor traditional Albanian cuisine, creating a nostalgic and vibrant dining experience.

Tirana's restaurants reflect the city's dynamic spirit, blending tradition with innovation. Whether you're savoring local specialties in a historic setting or enjoying international cuisine with a modern twist, the culinary landscape of Tirana promises a gastronomic journey filled with flavors, aromas, and memorable dining experiences.

Street Food in Tirana

Tirana's streets come alive with the aromas of delicious street food, offering a quick and flavorful way to experience local cuisine. Here are some popular street food options to savor:

1. Byrek

Address: Rruga 5 Maji 26a, Tirana, Albania

Savory Pastry: Byrek is a flaky pastry filled with various ingredients such as cheese, spinach, or minced meat. It's a popular and satisfying snack enjoyed throughout the day.

2. Qebapa

Address: Rruga Eshref Frasheri 76, Tirana, Albania
Phone Number: +355 69 830 0333

Grilled Delight: Qebapa consists of small, seasoned meat sausages, usually served with flatbread and diced onions. The aroma of grilling qebapa is a common sight in the streets of Tirana.

3. Kiosks and Bakeries

Quick Bites: Explore local kiosks and bakeries for quick bites like puff pastries, sandwiches, and stuffed burek. These are convenient options for those on the go.

4. Simit

Sesame-Crusted Bread: Similar to a bagel, simit is a circular bread covered in sesame seeds. It's often enjoyed plain or with toppings like jam or cheese.

5. Tavë Kosi Sandwich

Traditional Flavor on the Go: Tavë Kosi, a traditional Albanian dish with baked lamb and yogurt, is sometimes transformed into a sandwich for a portable and delicious street food option.

6. Grilled Corn (Misri i gëzuar)

Seasonal Delight: During the warmer months, you'll find street vendors grilling corn and serving it with a variety of toppings like salt, cheese, and spices.

Local Cuisine and Food Specialties

Albanian cuisine is a delightful blend of Mediterranean and Balkan flavors, showcasing fresh ingredients and traditional recipes. Here are some local dishes and specialties to savor in Tirana:

1. Tavë Kosi

National Dish: Tavë Kosi is a savory baked casserole featuring lamb or veal, rice, and yogurt. It's considered Albania's national dish, known for its rich and comforting flavors.

2. Fërgesë

Pepper and Cheese Delight: Fërgesë is a hearty dish made with green peppers, tomatoes, and local cheeses. It can be vegetarian or include meat, providing a burst of flavors.

3. Flija

Layered Pancake: Flija is a unique Albanian dish made by layering thin pancakes and baking them until they form a multi-layered cake. Usually served with honey or yogurt.

4. Tavë Dheu

Slow-Cooked Lamb: Tavë Dheu is a slow-cooked lamb dish, often prepared with vegetables and baked to perfection. It showcases the country's tradition of slow-cooking meat for tender results.

5. Baklava

Sweet Delight: Indulge in the sweet and sticky layers of baklava, a popular dessert made with layers of phyllo pastry, nuts, and honey or syrup.

Dietary Restrictions and Tips

For travelers with dietary restrictions or preferences, Tirana caters to a variety of culinary needs. Here are some tips and considerations:

1. Vegetarian and Vegan Options

- Vegetarian and vegan options are available in many restaurants, with a growing awareness of plant-based diets. Look for dishes featuring fresh vegetables, salads, and bean-based dishes.

2. Gluten-Free Choices

- Gluten-free options may be available in some establishments. Communicate your dietary needs with the restaurant staff, and they will often accommodate your requirements.

3. Seafood Selection

- Tirana is not a coastal city, so seafood options may be limited compared to coastal areas. However, some restaurants offer fresh seafood dishes, especially in the city center.

4. Communication with Staff

- Communicate any dietary restrictions or allergies with restaurant staff. They are usually accommodating and willing to provide information about ingredients and preparation methods.

5. Fresh Produce Markets

- Explore fresh produce markets like Pazari i Ri for a variety of fruits, vegetables, and local products. This allows you to customize your meals based on dietary preferences.

Popular Beverages and Nightlife

Tirana's nightlife scene is vibrant, with a variety of venues offering everything from traditional Albanian beverages to international cocktails. Here's a glimpse into the city's popular beverages and nightlife:

1. Raki

Traditional Spirit: Raki is a traditional Albanian spirit, often homemade and flavored with various fruits or herbs. For toasting and celebrating, it's a popular choice.

2. Café Culture

Relaxed Atmosphere: Tirana's café culture is thriving, with numerous establishments offering a relaxed atmosphere. Enjoy a cup of strong Albanian coffee or explore specialty coffee shops for a diverse range of brews.

3. Craft Beer Bars

Emerging Trend: Craft beer bars have become increasingly popular in Tirana, offering a variety of locally brewed and international craft beers. Explore these venues for a taste of the burgeoning beer culture.

4. Cocktail Bars

Mixology Magic: Cocktail bars in Tirana showcase skilled mixologists creating unique and inventive drinks. From classic cocktails to modern concoctions, the city's nightlife caters to diverse tastes.

5. Live Music Venues

Entertainment Hub: Tirana boasts live music venues that cover a spectrum of genres. Enjoy performances by local and international artists in settings ranging from intimate jazz clubs to lively concert halls.

6. Rooftop Bars

Panoramic Views: Experience Tirana's skyline from rooftop bars that offer panoramic views of the city. It's an ideal setting for evening drinks and relaxation.

7. Nightclubs

Late-Night Entertainment: Tirana's nightclubs come alive in the late hours, offering dance floors, DJ sets, and a vibrant atmosphere. The city's nightlife is diverse, catering to various tastes and preferences.

Tirana's culinary landscape, street food offerings, and nightlife scene reflect the city's dynamic and evolving character. Whether you're savoring local specialties, exploring the café culture, or enjoying the energetic nightlife, Tirana invites you to indulge in a diverse and memorable culinary journey.

CHAPTER SEVEN

Practical Information

Local Etiquette and Customs in Tirana

Understanding local etiquette and customs is key to a respectful and enjoyable experience in Tirana. Important aspects to consider include:

Greetings and Politeness
Greetings often involve a handshake, and close friends may exchange kisses on both cheeks. It's customary to address people using formal titles unless invited to use first names.

Respect for Elders

In Albanian culture, respecting elders is deeply ingrained. When entering a room, it's common to greet the oldest person first as a sign of respect.

Hospitality

Albanians are known for their warm hospitality. If invited to someone's home, it's customary to bring a small gift, such as flowers or sweets, as a token of appreciation.

Dress Modestly in Religious Sites

When visiting mosques or churches, dress modestly. Women may be required to cover their heads in some religious sites.

Mealtime Etiquette

Wait for the host or eldest person to start the meal before beginning to eat. It's polite to try a bit of everything and express appreciation for the food.

Shoes Off Indoors

It's customary to remove your shoes when entering someone's home. This practice extends to some traditional restaurants and guesthouses.

Gift-Giving Culture

Gift-giving is common during holidays and celebrations. It's the thought that counts, so a small, thoughtful gift is appreciated.

Tipping Practices

Tipping is appreciated but not always mandatory. In restaurants, rounding up the bill or leaving around 10% is customary. Tipping is also common for services like taxis and tour guides.

Local Phrases and Words for Travelers in Tirana

Engaging with the local language adds a personal touch to your travel experience in Tirana. While many locals in urban areas may speak English, showing an effort to use Albanian phrases is appreciated. Here's a guide to some useful local phrases and words:

1. Greetings

- *Tungjatjeta* (toon-jat-yet-a): Hello

- *Mirëmëngjes* (meer-em-eng-yes): Good morning

- *Mirëdita* (meer-eh-dee-ta): Good day

- *Mirëmbrema* (meer-em-breh-ma): Good evening

- *Natën e mirë* (na-ten eh meer): Good night

2. Courtesy Phrases

- *Ju lutem* (yoo loo-tem): Please

- *Faleminderit* (fah-le-meen-deh-reet): Thank you

- *Ju falem nderit shumë* (yoo fah-lehm nde-reet shu-meh): Thank you very much

- *Më falni* (muh fahl-nee): Excuse me / I'm sorry

3. Basic Communication
- *Po* (poh): Yes

- *Jo* (yo): No

- *Si jeni?* (see yeh-nee): How are you?

- *Mirë, faleminderit* (meer-eh, fah-le-meen-deh-reet): Well, thank you

- *Si quheni?* (see ch-oo-heh-nee): What's your name?

4. Direction and Location

- *Ku është...?* (koo uh-sht uh): Where is...?

- *Drejtimi* (drey-tee-mee): Direction

- *Afër* (ah-fer): Near

- *Larg* (larg): Far

5. Food and Dining

- *Faleminderit për ushqimin* (fah-le-meen-deh-reet per oosh-chi-min): Thank you for the food

- *Një kafe, ju lutem* (nyuh kah-feh, yoo loo-tem): A coffee, please

- *Hesht* (hesht): Delicious

- *Llogaritni, ju lutem* (lo-ga-ree-tee, yoo loo-tem): The bill, please

6. Common Phrases

- *Mirupafshim* (meer-oo-paf-shim): Goodbye

- *Tung* (toong): Goodbye (informal)

- *Mirë se vini* (meer eh vee-nee): Welcome

- *Po mire* (po mee-re): I'm fine

- *Jam i humbur* (yam ee hoom-boor): I am lost

7. Travel Essentials

- *Ku është stacioni i autobusëve?* (koo uh-sht eh stah-tsee-oh-nee ee ah-oo-boos-eh-veh): Where is the bus station?

- *Sa kushton biletë për...?* (sah koo-sh-ton bee-leh-te per): How much is a ticket to...?

- *Ku është emergjenca?* (koo uh-sht eh eh-mehr-gyen-tsah): Where is the emergency?

Numbers 1-10

Albanian: *Një* (nyuh) / *Dy* (duh) / *Tre* (tray) / *Katër* (kah-ter) / *Pesë* (peh-seh) / *Gjashtë* (gyasht) / *Shtatë* (shtah-tuh) / *Tetë* (teht) / *Nëntë* (nun-tuh) / *Dhjetë* (th-yet)

Learning these phrases not only enhances your travel experience but also demonstrates respect for the local culture. Most Albanians appreciate the effort, even if your pronunciation is not perfect. So, don't hesitate to try out these phrases and enjoy the warm reception from the people of Tirana!

Communication and Connectivity

Staying connected and communicating in Tirana is relatively easy, thanks to modern infrastructure. Here are some essential points:

1. Mobile Networks

Tirana has reliable mobile networks. Local SIM cards are available for purchase, providing cost-effective options for data and calling.

2. Internet Access

In cafes, hotels and public spaces, Wi-Fi is widely available. Most accommodations offer complimentary internet access.

3. Language Considerations

While Albanian is the official language, English is commonly spoken in urban areas, especially by the younger population and those in the service industry.

4. Currency and Payment

The official currency is the Albanian lek (ALL). Credit cards are widely accepted in hotels, restaurants, and larger shops, but it's advisable to carry some cash for smaller establishments.

5. Post Offices

Post offices are available for mailing letters and packages. Most post offices offer additional services, including currency exchange.

6. Time Zone

Tirana operates on Central European Time (CET), UTC+1.

Understanding the local language and communication norms, along with having access to connectivity options, ensures a smooth and enjoyable experience while exploring Tirana and engaging with the local culture.

CONCLUSION

As you prepare to conclude your journey in Tirana, let's wrap up your travel guide with final tips, sustainable travel practices, and leaving feedback for a memorable and responsible travel experience.

Final Tips for Travel

Immerse in Local Culture
- Embrace the local customs, try traditional dishes, and engage with locals to truly immerse yourself in the rich culture of Tirana.

Explore Beyond the City Center
- Venture into the neighborhoods beyond the city center to discover hidden gems, local markets, and

authentic experiences that may not be immediately apparent in tourist hubs.

Stay Flexible

- Be open to spontaneity. Sometimes the best experiences happen when you deviate from your planned itinerary and go with the flow.

Respect Nature

Whether hiking in Mount Dajti or strolling by the Artificial Lake, be mindful of nature. Follow marked trails, avoid littering, and contribute to the preservation of the city's natural beauty.

Capture Memories Responsibly

Capture the beauty of Tirana but do so respectfully. Ask for permission before taking photos of locals, especially in more intimate settings, and avoid intrusive behavior.

Learn Basic Local Phrases

While English is widely spoken, learning a few basic phrases in Albanian can go a long way in building connections and showing respect for the local language.

Sustainable Travel Practices

Support Local Businesses
- Opt for locally-owned accommodations, eateries, and shops. This not only contributes to the local economy but also provides a more authentic experience.

Use Public Transportation
- Reduce your carbon footprint by utilizing public transportation or walking whenever possible. Tirana has a well-developed bus system, and many attractions are easily accessible on foot.

Minimize Single-Use Plastics

- Be conscious of your environmental impact by minimizing single-use plastics. Carry a reusable water bottle and shopping bag to reduce waste during your travels.

Respect Wildlife and Natural Spaces

- Whether exploring national parks or urban green spaces, respect wildlife and follow designated paths. Avoid disrupting ecosystems and contribute to the preservation of natural habitats.

Conserve Water and Energy

- Practice water and energy conservation in your accommodations. Turn off lights and appliances when not in use, and be mindful of water usage, especially in areas with water scarcity.

Offset Your Carbon Footprint

- Consider carbon offset programs to balance the environmental impact of your travel. Many organizations offer opportunities to invest in sustainability projects.

Leaving Feedback

Online Reviews

- Share your experiences on travel platforms, providing constructive feedback to help other travelers and giving credit to businesses that uphold high standards.

Social Media

- Share your favorite moments on social media, tagging local establishments and using location-based hashtags. Your positive posts can contribute to the promotion of responsible tourism.

Direct Communication

- If you had exceptional service or encountered any challenges, consider providing direct feedback to the businesses involved. This direct communication allows them to improve and grow.

Community Engagement

- Engage with travel forums and communities to share insights and learn from other travelers. Your experiences can be valuable for those planning their trips to Tirana.

Leaving Tirana with a sense of appreciation for its culture, a commitment to sustainable practices, and thoughtful feedback will not only enhance your own travel memories but also contribute to the well-being of this dynamic and welcoming city. Safe travels!

APPENDIX

Alphabetical List of Topics and Locations Covered in this Guide

Topics Covered

Accommodation Options in Tirana

Banks in Tirana

Best Time to Visit Tirana

Cultural Experience

Detailed Accommodation Options in Tirana

Detailed Maps and Key Areas

Locations Covered

Dajti Ekspres

Dajti National Park

Era Restaurant

Era Vila 1928

Farka Lake

Grand Park of Tirana

Juvenilja

Mullixhiu

National Historical Museum

Oda

Pellumbas Cave

Pellumbas Restaurant

Pazari i Ri (New Bazaar)

Petrela Castle

Salt

Serendipity Wine and Coffee Bar

Skanderbeg Square

Tanners' Bridge

The Pyramid of Tirana

Tirana International Airport Nënë Tereza

Tirana Zoo

Tirana's Clock Tower

Tirana's University of Arts

Tregu i Madh (Main Market)

Tregu i Ri (New Bazaar)

Tregu Peshkut (Fish Market)

Tropikal Resort

University of Arts

Wilson Square

THE END!
HAPPY READING AND SAFE
JOURNEY!

John P. Wade cares!

Tirana International Hotel
& Conference Centre

Rruga e ~~Dibës~~

Dibës

Printed in Great Britain
by Amazon